C

Foreword	
Mirror, Mirror	
A Fairytale	6
Winterwald	9
The Rescue	11
Prayer to the Bright One	13
Seeker of the Grail	15
Eva	17
I Belong to You	19
Gather the Tribe	21
He Lives in Truth	23
Aurora	25
Shadow's Song	27
Prayer to the Thunderer	29
Rolling Waves	31
Momentary Rapture	33
The Blood Gift	35
Celestial Blessings	37
The Poet and the Oak	38
Light Beyond the Grave	43
Awaken Teutonia!	45
We Transcend Time	47
Lord of the Northern Night	49
Love and Death on Halloween	51
Desire's Yoke	53
The Labyrinth	55
Artwork credits	56

Foreword

It's been about two years since the publication of Pagan Poems Volume II. A lot has happened in my own life over these past few years, and big things are going on in the wider world that affects the lives and emotions of myself and my readers. But, the addage is somewhat true that the more things change the more they remain the same.

I find myself still on the continuous search for what is real. My spiritual journey has only strengthened my faith in our Goddess of the Dawn and she has been an illuminating force in my consciousness. But, with knowledge comes sometimes even more hardship. In this moment, I find myself carrying the hefty weight of those who know too much. The world is on the verge of great change, but we are still fettered by the forces of those who would keep us shackled.

In my *naïveté*, I endeavored to bring the fruits of historical research to an audience not ready to face what has been hidden. And, so, not knowing where to go next, I dove back into the realm of poesie. Reality is heavy stuff. But, we are a race that has always reveled in the beauty of art. Painting with words, I hope, provides a salve for some of the stresses of the modern world. It always lifts my heavy heart when I sift through centuries of European artwork to illustrate these projects. It reminds me of the strength and beauty we are capable of as a people. I hope that in these pages will you find a respite from storm.

Carolyn Emerick

November, 2019

Mirror, Mirror

Once before, when I was free,
the sun shone through mine eyes.
The world was but a candy-coated
spring garden of delights.

O' then did I believe in love,
and, thus, I had it, too.
But that was shown a fickle farce.
Is there nothing that is true?

Ephemeral are all things,
and all good things must pass.
When it all has turned to dust,
tell me, what will last?

Mirror, mirror, tell me, please,
what cloud does block their vision?
And how it is we came to live
in a world full of illusion?

A Fairytale

Hurled violently into the wood
where many monsters lurked,
the princess set off down the path
where predators did stalk.

A sudden noise, a rush of wind,
scared her to the bones.
But, a supernatural voice rang out
and said she's not alone.

She met a beggar, and a witch,
and a ring of fairies, too.
They gave her tests and trials
to prove her heart was true.

And then she came upon a well
where dwelled three golden waifs.
They cast the runes and read the signs
as her Wyrd they did appraise.

One by one they raised their heads
kenning looks upon their faces.
My dear, please no longer fear,
your journey's not been wasted.

And, so the princess stood and then
she held her head up high.
When she set back on the road
she was met with a surprise.

For in her path she saw a form
that she knew from way back when.
The Elfin King stood waiting, and
said "hello there, my old friend."

Reaching out, he clasped her hand
and instantly she knew.
Her destiny had manifest;
fated fairytales come true.

Winterwald

Crackling leaves
and the creaking of trees,
a hawk flies just overhead.
There's no other sound
save the steps of my hound,
in the forest winter-dead.

A flash of brown
bounds a way down
across the deserted path.
Vaguely we hear
the wind-rush of deer
making me stifle a laugh.

The forest is still
and will be until
the Bright One brings forth the light.
But here in the dark
we gather our thoughts
in contemplation this long night.

The Rescue

This world is raging like a storm
and I've weathered it alone.
Cold and damp and shivering,
exhaustion overwhelmed my bones.

Tossed into the violent waves
which hurled me to and fro.
Waterlogged, I couldn't breathe,
currents pulling from below.

Then the Fates they intervened
and placed me gently on the shore.
In a haze I heard a voice
that made me thirst for more.

Tribulations I'd endured
had taken a great toll...
But his words into my ears
were like a salve on my frayed soul.

And slowly I grew stronger
as my spirit began to mend.
And if the Fates be good and true,
I won't brave storms alone again.

Prayer to the Bright One

Goddess good and goddess bright,
please look down on me tonight.
Bring me luck, and bring me wealth,
bring me happiness and health.

I feel your presence watching me
with every birdsong in the trees.
And the sun that shines so bright
warms us with your loving light.

Sometimes when I'm feeling low,
I see the saplings start to grow.
And flowers colorful and bright
say that things will be alright.

Thank you for new life each Spring,
for the birds whose song does ring.
With grace beyond the ken of men,
you show us life begins again.

Seeker of the Grail

Dost thou take the time to see
what is right before thine eyes?
For when the fleeting magic flees,
there may be no reprise.

If thou tryest, thou can learn
how to see anew.
But this challenge comes not free,
a price paid by only you.

So step into the gauntlet,
and run with all thy might.
Use all thy strength and courage,
don't cower from the fight.

Break down every barrier
that blocks thee from the truth.
Cultivate thy fortitude
if dark secrets thou dost sooth.

If thou be good and thou be strong,
and useth all thy wits,
visible thy path will be.
But thou mustn't quit!

Grueling though the road might be,
stand strong and see it through.
For at the end a treasure waits;
a *sangreal* made for you.

Eva

Long and graceful elegance
like a willowy lean stem
of a fragrant gentle flower
with sharp wits at the helm.

She was such a thing of beauty
that made other women green.
But she walked with such poise
that the world has nary seen.

Blessed were we who gathered round
warmed by her bright light.
Her spirit will linger long among
those who see her star each night.

I Belong to You

Speak to me in rhythm,
and speak to me in rhyme.
For when we speak together,
suspended is all time.

Transmitted through the ether
on an energetic plane.
Your soul touches mine
in a way that isn't sane.

We're connected in a universe
that others do not know.
For we met not on this Earth,
but in the land of souls.

You speak a gentle cadence
that others cannot hear.
But the wisdom that you speak
is music to my ears.

Though we're separated,
my heart is ever true.
No one else could resonate,
for I belong to you.

Gather the Tribe

Behold, the lady doth call out
with a voice that's clear and true,
to the Folk with ears to hear,
she calleth out to you!

Hark! And hear the pipes do ring
like crystal through the ether.
We had been blind and lost before,
but now our Folk do gather.

Our tribe is scattered round the world
and many, they are lost.
But, others will gladly pay the price
to succeed at any cost.

To our kith and to our kin,
to our cousin clans worldwide.
Strengthen your backbone and resolve,
do not shrink and hide!

Hear the call and heed the voice
that rallies for our kin.
The battle ahead will be intense,
but together, we will win!

He Lives in Truth

He lives with honor and in truth.
He walks with dignity and couth.
His wisdom is beyond his years,
    far surpassing of his peers.

But it's his soul that speaks to me,
and his heart that sets mine free.
His spirit touches deep inside,
and I've lost instinct to hide

I want to give myself to him,
in every way, not just a whim.
Live for his pleasure, and to please.
For, without him, I can't be me.

Aurora

Hail the rising of the Dawn!
She breaks the ice and brings the warmth.
She brings the light and starts each day,
chases dark nightmares away.

Though, legends say the maiden sleeps
inside the thorny castle keep.
Her lover faces dragon fire
to rouse the maid we all admire.

For fair wee babe received a curse,
the three Wyrd Sisters did reverse.
Rather than eternal slumber,
by love's kiss, our Rose recovers.

Gallant hero, fulfill thine oath.
Save fair maid, thine own betrothed.
When she wakes, she lifts the veil.
She brings the sun and stops the hail.

With radiance of glowing sun,
our maiden makes the dark ones run!
She brings the buds of new life, too.
May Aurora's blessings shine on you.

Shadow's Song

My words were hitherto unmatched,
my soul fly-freeing and detached.
Admirers have come and gone,
and I have listened to their song.

But no one else has met my mind,
keeps up with me, leaves me behind.
And no one else has spoke to me
with a depth that sets me free.

He is everything I've waited for,
his value set above all score.
But disappointed in life I've been,
and so I might miss out on him.

If the stars be real and true,
blazing against the sky so blue,
what unfolds is what will be…
I pray that he'll belong to me.

Prayer to the Thunderer

God of Thunder, God of might,
give us strength to win this fight.
God of lighting, God of storm,
strike down those who do us harm.

Though timeless foes we face today,
it's not our first go in this fray.
When the cross came with the sword,
you helped us keep at bay the hordes.

Swarthy priests looked down with scorn,
and burned alive our native-born.
You gave us inner strength to stand
and not be crushed by enemy hands.

And now we must prepare again,
for all of our tribes' children.
We need you more than e'er before
as Mordor's orcs invade our shores.

Mighty Thunor, to you we pray,
please aid us when we're in the fray.
With faith and truth we will prevail.
O' mighty Thor, to you we hail!

Rolling Waves

When the waves are rolling
and it's difficult to swim,
I'll always be beside you,
it's a promise, not a whim.
For the storm is ever raging,
and it gets difficult to see.
But, I won't give up and sink
because you are here with me.

When the hard and heavy waves
crash and roll and bend and rise,
and then the roaring raging wind
rips through the darkened skies,
I do not fear or tremble,
for I am always safe and dry.
You are here beside me,
your steady words do ease my mind.

And if the knowing faithful Fates
be ever good and wise and true,
and if the eternal swirling ocean's
waves are the brightest blue,
I call out into the heavens,
to the Morning Star above,
and swear with my whole heart
no one else could have my love.

Momentary Rapture

Enveloped by feeling,
and enveloped by sound.
Lost within vibration,
that wraps you all around.

A symphony of magic,
cacophony of noise.
And this rush of energy
will chase away the void.

In the darkest depths of night
when others do not wake,
that's when everything is vibrant
and meaning saturates.

The Blood Gift

The air is crisp and cool,
and the moon is beaming bright,
lighting up the clouds against
the velvet sky tonight.

And I feel alive with wonder,
and I feel alive with light.
For I feel the effervescence
that is alive this night.

For we tap into the source
of our ancestral might.
If we can read the energy,
then we receive the sight.

When we see then we can know
what is true and right.
Our ancestors infuse our blood;
emboldened for the fight.

And tonight I gaze upon
celestial white on blue.
I know that I am not alone,
for I'm in this fight with you.

Celestial Blessings

'O Vakarine, daughter of the night,
harness the past to set things right.
Bind that which has inflicted harm,
to ready for thy sister's warmth.

For, hark! I hear the sounding of horns
heralding the Lady of the Morn!
Her arrival signals the end of strife,
for Ausrine is the Bringer of New Life.

And, when little saplings begin to grow,
have faith and hope, for inside we know
that Saule, the Sun, Mother of all
is sending her blessings. To us they befall.

The Poet and the Oak

The poet has her back against
the Willow's gentle form,
seeking out protection from
the onslaught of the storm.

The Willow tries, and does its best,
but it bends and turns.
The poet's work is jarred because
the Willow isn't firm.

And so, the poet must step out
into blowing, furious winds.
Eyes set with determination,
a shamanic journey begins.

Wobbling that first step may be,
she's careful not to falter.
Noisy, though, these winds do seem,
her course will not be altered.

Swirling whirling tempest blasts
are filled with ghastly voices.
But nary will our daring lass
let ghouls decide her choices.

Soul-searching blood-memory deep,
calling the gods and her ancestors,
our poet finds an inner strength
to resist the misdirectors.

New voices her thoughts can hear
echoing from times long past.
Archetypal forces whisper,
that this hurricane won't last.

With newfound strength, she sojourns on,
believing every word here spoke.
And when the fog is lifted up,
she meets the strong gaze of the Oak.

"Daughter," says he, with knowing tones,
"come shelter 'neath my branches.
Thy journey's only just begun,
though you've faced so many lances.

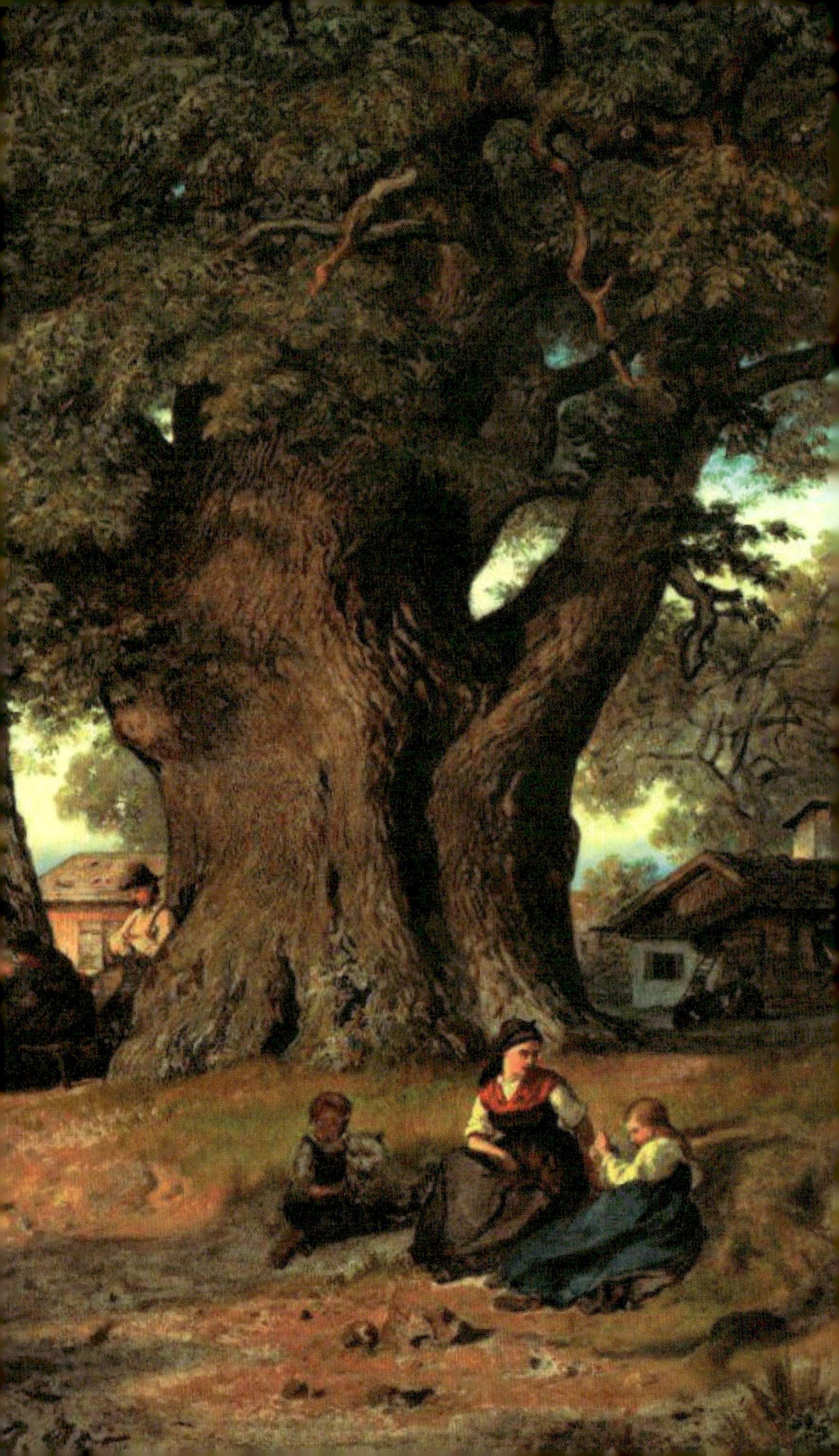

Lean your weary back against
my rough but steady bark.
Breathe the clean and healing air,
listen deeply to the larks.

My roots they reach deep down in Earth;
she is mine and your own mother.
My branches stretch into blue skies,
home to our feathered brothers.

The storms will rage and they will ebb,
but Mother Nature reigns eternal.
Honor her and draw her strength
when you're caught in the inferno."

Our poet thanked the wizened Oak
for truth transcending ages;
for healing strength and courage
fused with knowledge of the sages.

And when she felt refreshed enough
to continue her life's quest,
she now possessed the tools to
elicit future's manifest.

Just like the Oak, the poet has
roots running deep into the past.
Her hopes and dreams are branches that
will not give up our land so fast.

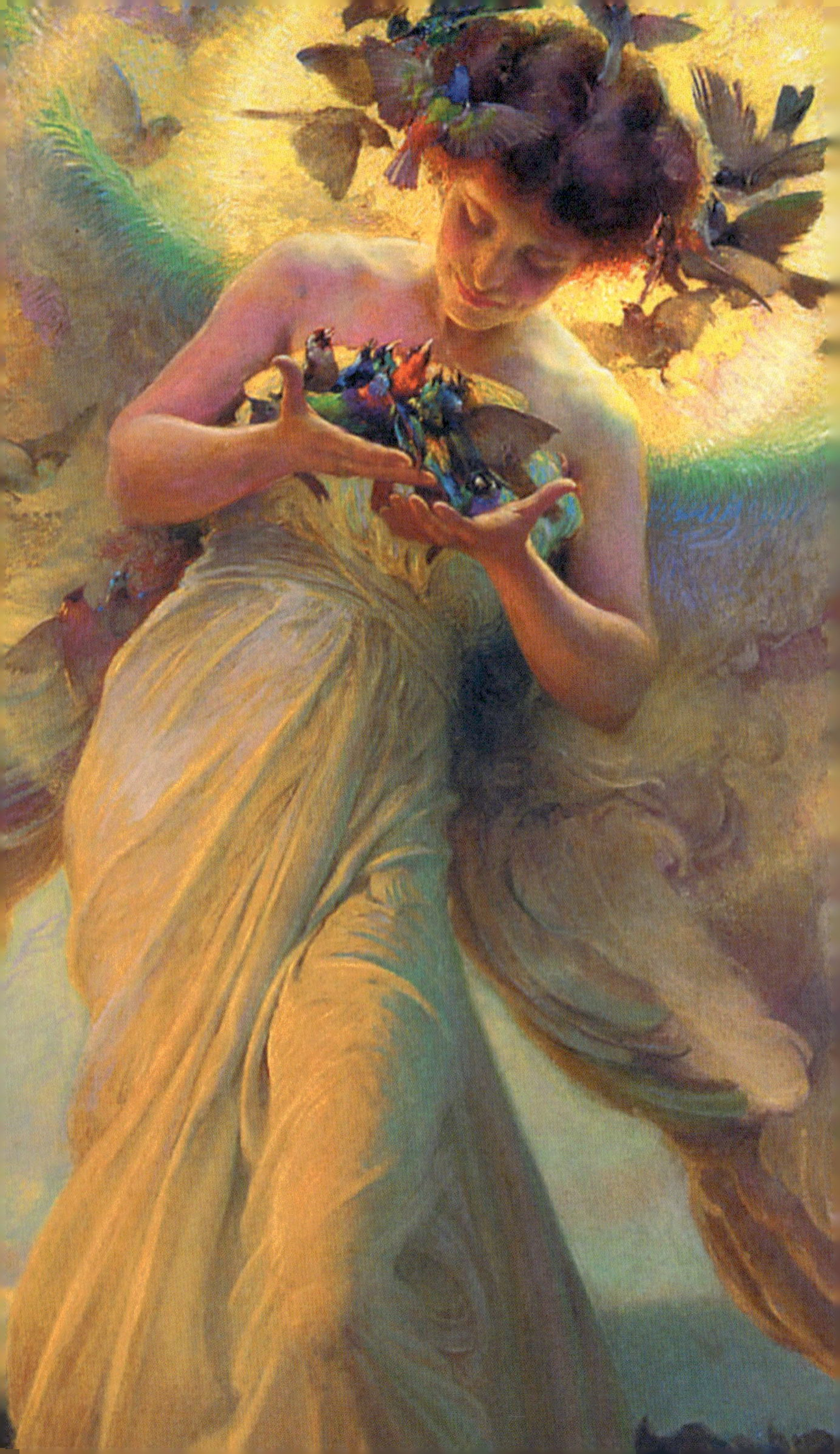

Light Beyond the Grave

You've always been my candle
when the dark of night crept in.
And you kept me warm and dry
when cold waves were a'crashing.

My chubby infant fingers
tracing veins upon your hands.
Your voice of strong support
and sometimes reprimand.

I thought I wouldn't carry on
when they placed you in the ground.
But no sooner had your body gone
than I felt your spirit all around.

You sent me words of love
like you always did before.
And that you'll always be a lighthouse
to guide me toward the shore.

With sign and symbol and a song
your voice rings through somehow.
Spirit lives on after death and
I have a fairy godmother, now.

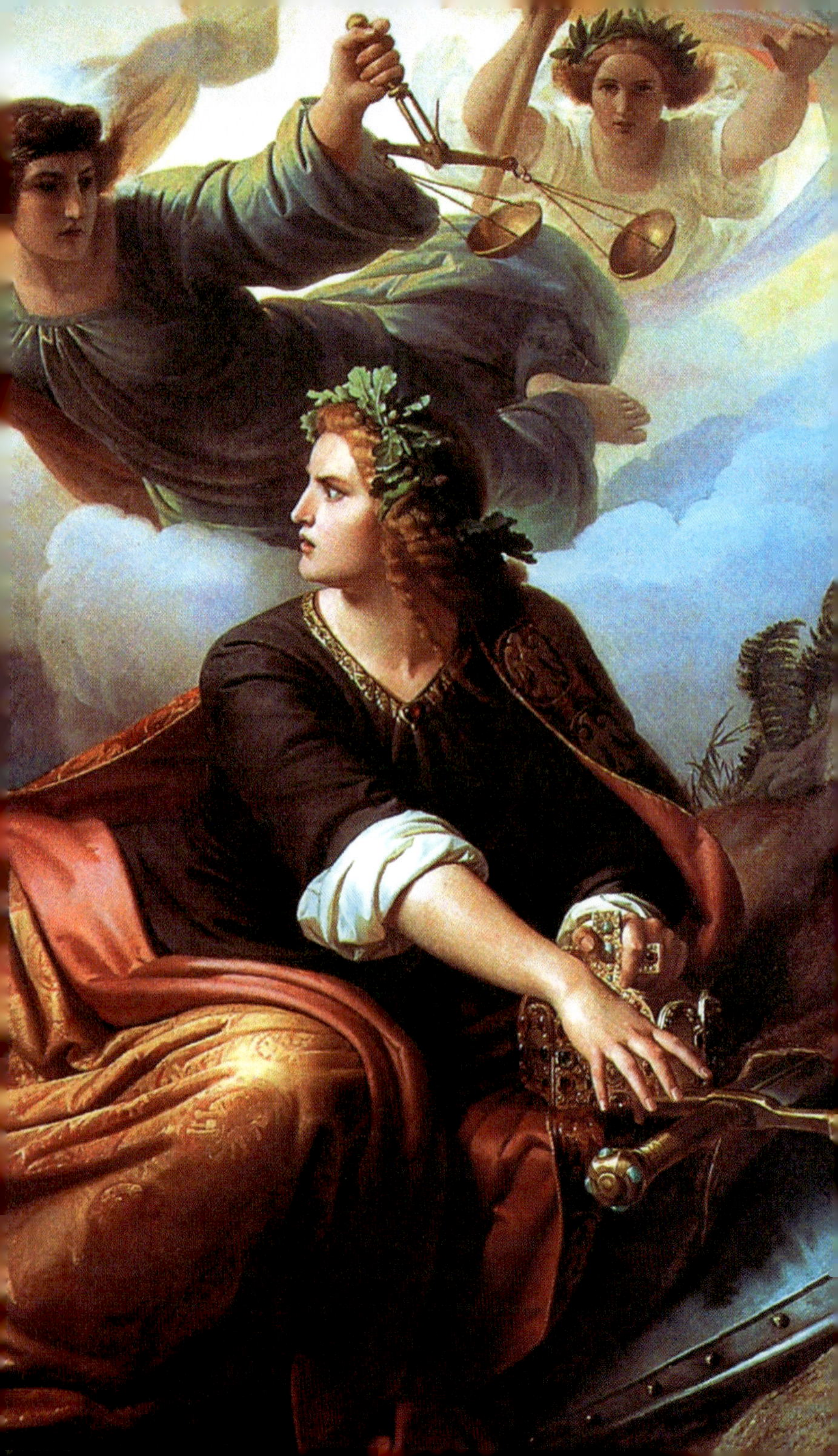

Awaken Teutonia!

They hurl out words like "bigot,"
as our children field abuse.
They demand we welcome in
the entire world's refuse.

They say that we're the devil
of the very world we built!
And then attempt to shame us
with "white privilege" and guilt.

Bearded imams proudly preach
for the mass rape of our women.
While social leaders call out
for the slaughter of white children.

These things are not imagined,
they are happening right now.
With most of us in shock,
and simply asking "how?"

How is it that it's come to this?
Where have our leaders been?
Their failure to protect us
has been their gravest sin.

So now the Folk must rise up
take our fate into our hands.
Dismantle the establishment,
now we must seize command!

We will not go silent into the night,
like sheep sent to their slaughter.
The Northern Wolf will show his might
to protect our sons and daughters!

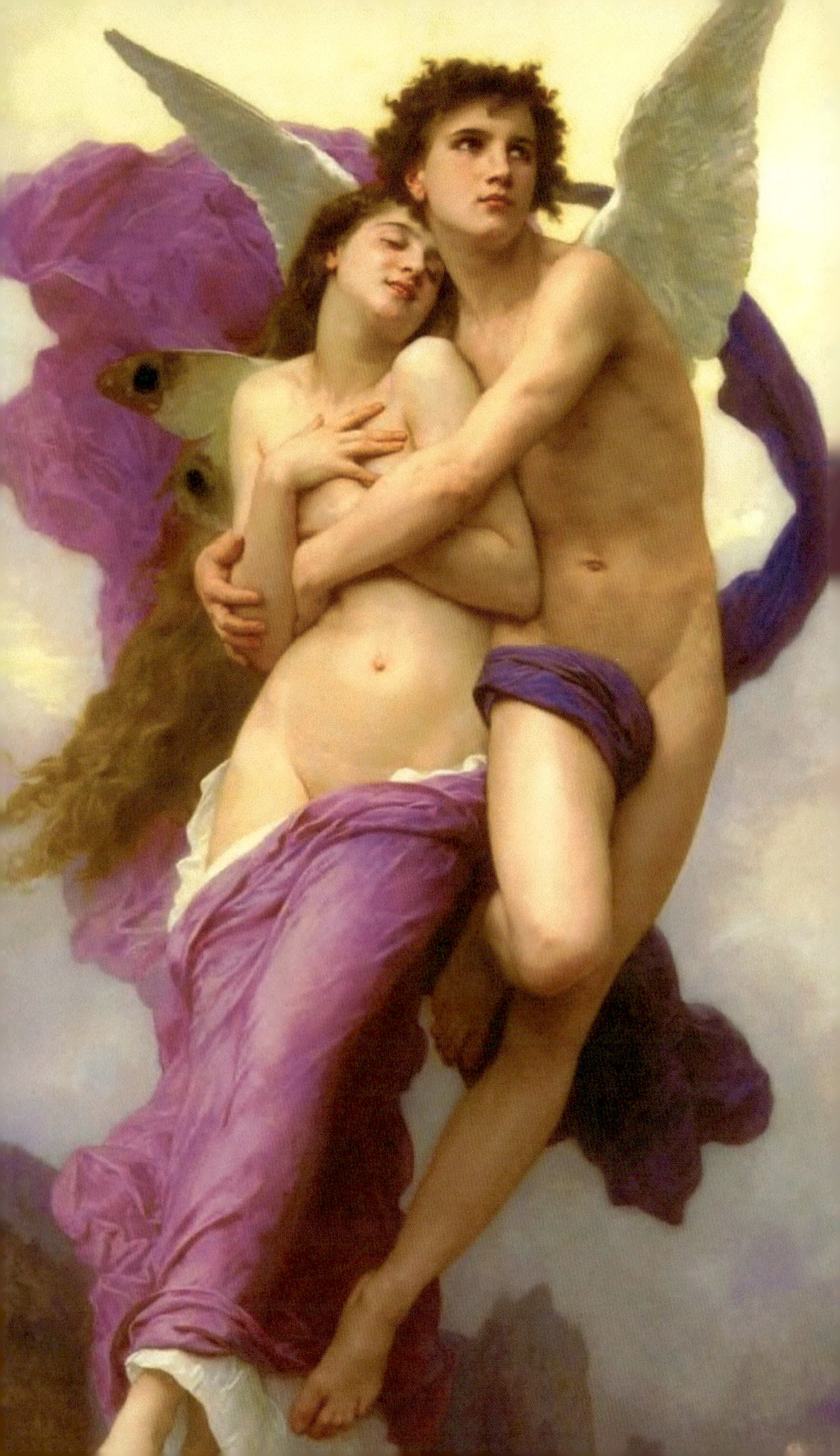

We Transcend Time

You and I,
we transcend time
For thou art mine,
and I am thine.
Just as sure
as stars do shine
I am thine,
and thou art mine.
And even when
the world doth grind,
thou art mine
and I am thine.
And you shall never
ache nor pine
For I am thine,
and thou art mine.
Though sometimes you
might need remind,
we will reach
the highest climes.
For I am yours,
and you are mine
And you and I,
we transcend time.

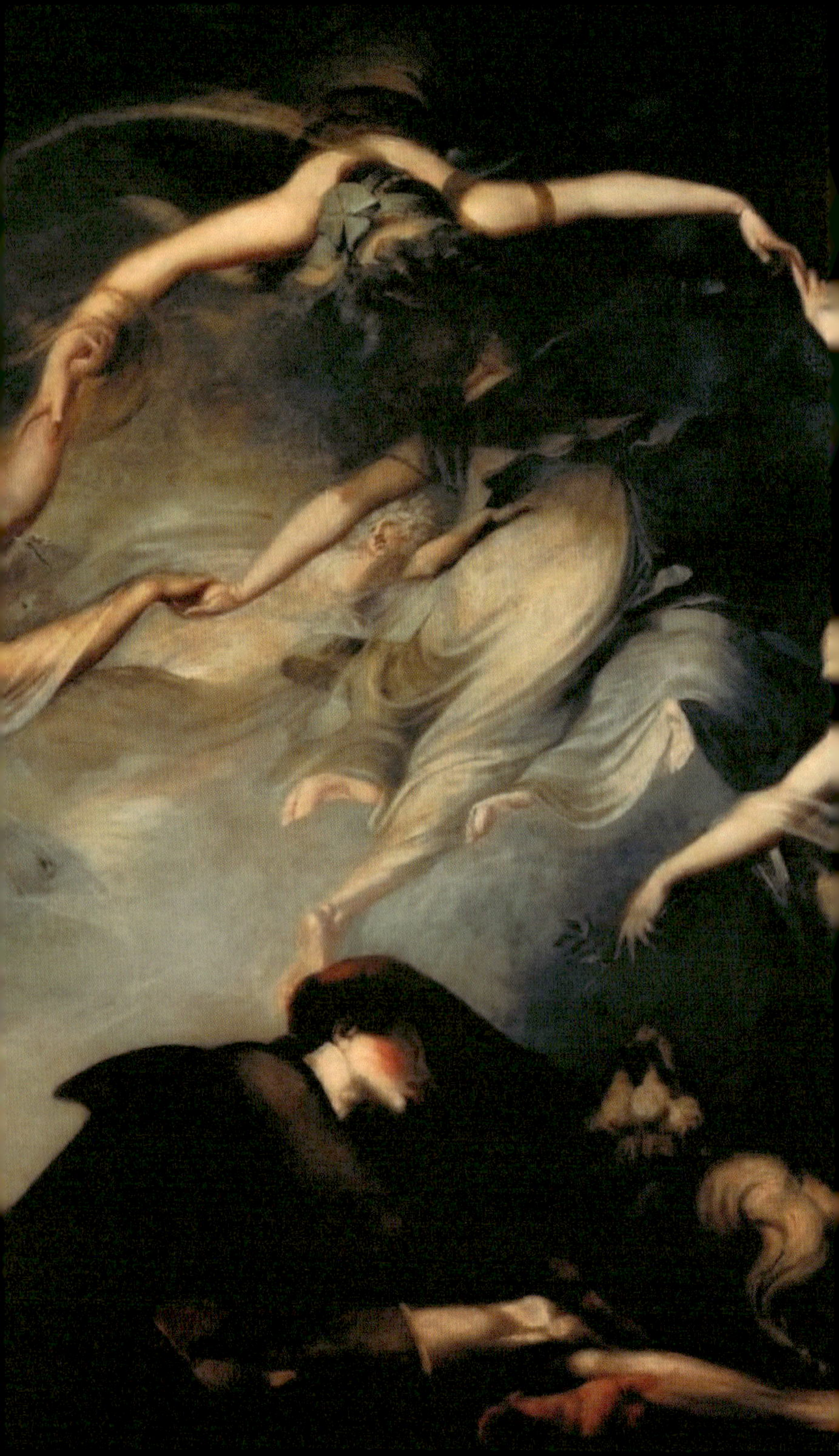

Lord of the Northern Night

Máni shines his bright beams down,
    while we're fast asleep.
Unaware though we may be,
a solemn vigil he doth keep.

His children slumber 'round the world,
    and most are far from home.
Engulfed by the frigid night,
please, do know we're not alone.

We are scattered by the four winds
    to new nations artificial.
Máni's folk are dreaming of
something almost sacrificial.

We dream of homelands far away,
    and remember our ancestors.
We're grateful for the journey's took
to escape from their oppressors.

We thank you, Máni, for the night,
    and the solitude it brings.
Thank you for the velvet skies
laced with silver fairies' wings.

And when we wake up in the morn,
    refreshed and made anew,
we can handle come what may;
thirst quenched by morning dew.

Máni's children, sleep and dream
    of a future shining bright.
Refresh our lands, both old and new,
wake up to our birthright!

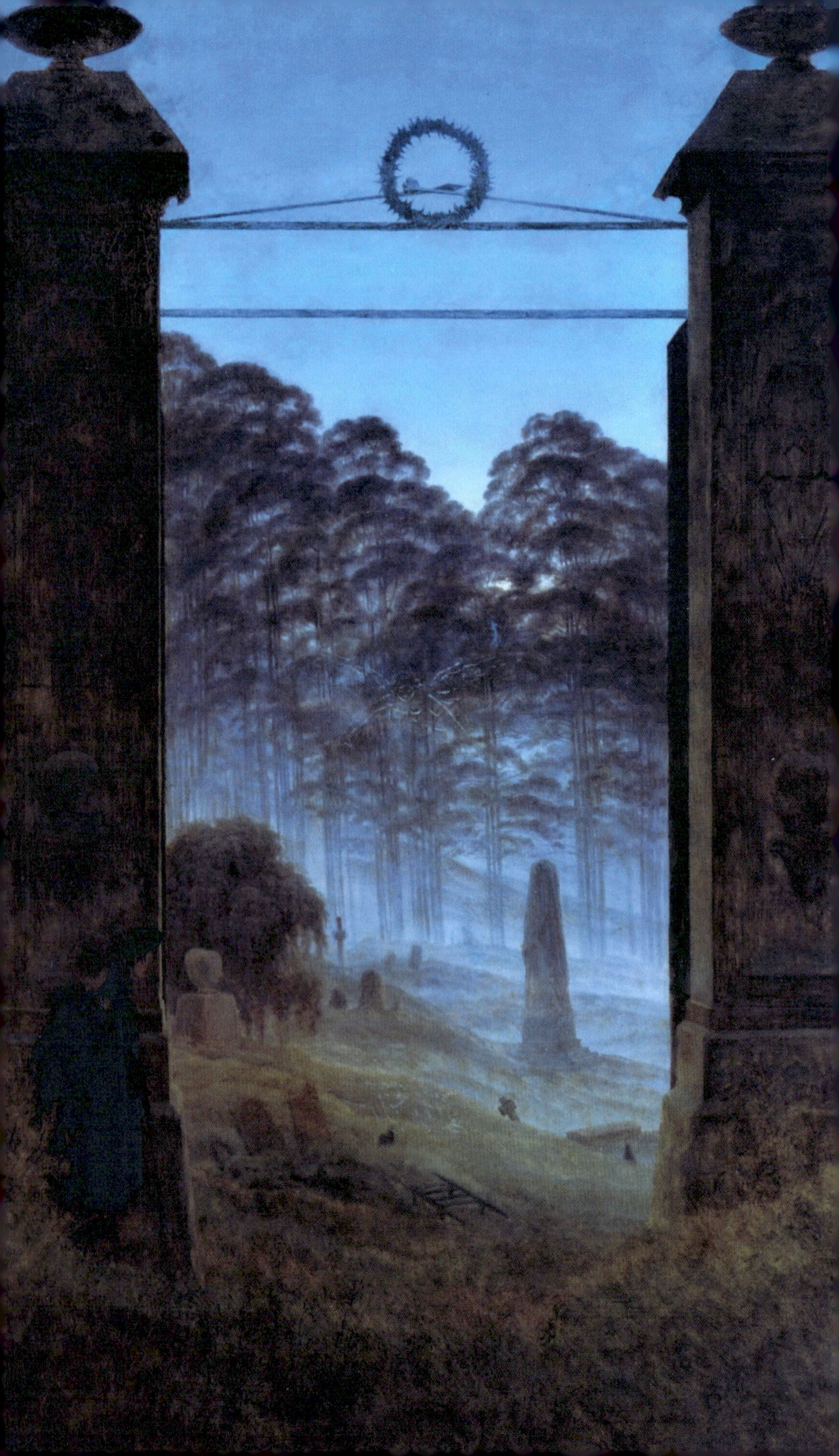

Love and Death on Halloween

Love and death on Halloween,
souls deceased are seen once again.
We feel great joy, and also lament
remembering our dead on Samhain.

While the skeleton trees are rustling
to the touch of the howling wind,
Together we bare our broken hearts
made light by joyous sin.

Ethereal eyes pierce our sad souls,
those lost who cannot return.
Tonight the ghosts are on parole.
So raise a glass, together we mourn.

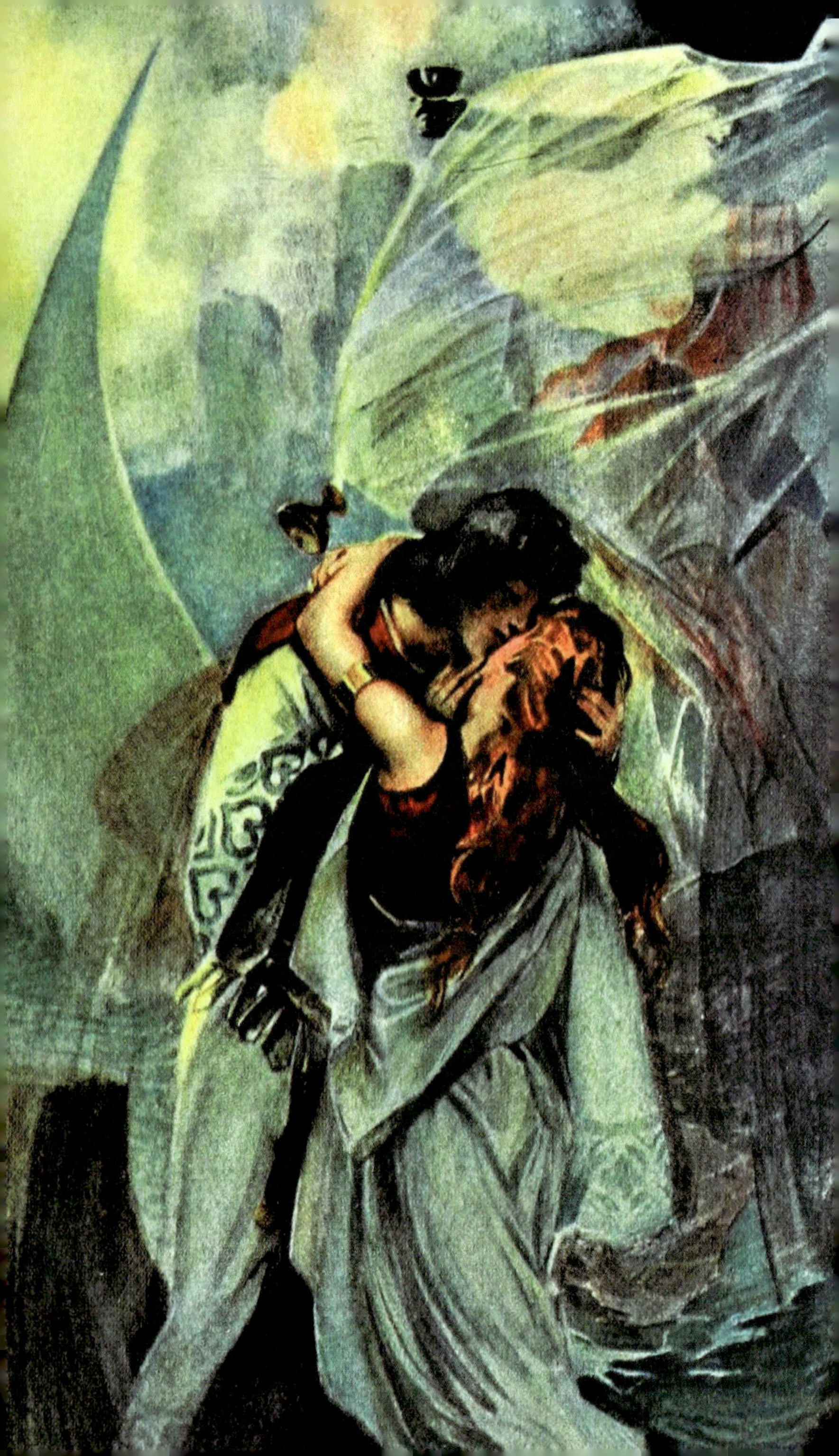

Desire's Yoke

O' Ladies who do weave my wyrd
at the sacred well,
I pray to you my voice be heard
if my secrets I do tell.

Please, hear the yearning of my plea
if I bare to you my heart.
Ladies, end my misery
by casting Cupid's dart.

Let it strike the one on whom
mine eyes they are fixated.
Kindle such a hunger strong
that without me can't be sated.

Weavers of my destiny,
to you I do appeal.
Please, grant a love that fleeteth not,
but one that's truly real.

Let him see my inner heart
and feel my sacred soul.
Please fuse our bond together tight
so we may make one whole.

Mistress Norns, and the Disir,
the matrons of our Folk,
give to me my destined love
and together we'll be yoked.

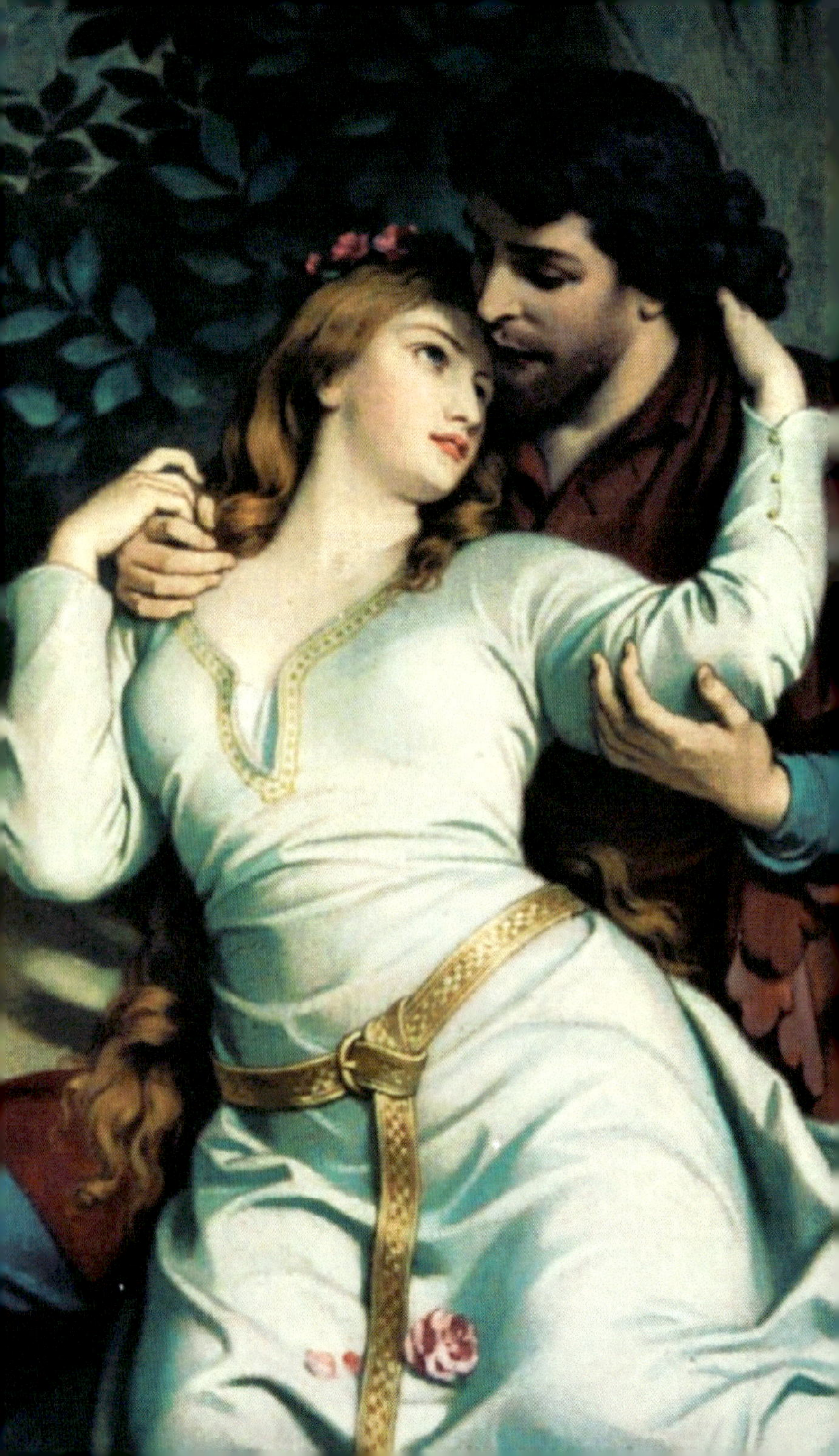

The Labyrinth

So she sleepeth still and deep
in cavern dim and dark;
wherefore none do ever creep
and never chimes the lark.

In her slumber comes to mind
remembers of days past,
with always sneaking reprimand
for things failed to forecast.

Through her hazy sleeping gaze,
her eyes fell upon a friend.
She'd been trapped inside this maze,
but now she saw him at the end.

Reaching forth his steady arms,
he pulled her to his side.
With countenance of strength and charm,
she no longer had to hide.

My bonny lass, you'll come with me
to castle yonder there,
where the larks sing in the trees
and the fox doth chase the hare.

And each morn, the sun will shine
upon our fair wee bairns.
Forever, now, thou art mine,
thy blue eyes and gold hair.

Artwork Credits

4   Water Nymph, Sergey Panasenko-Mikhalkin

7   Hesperus, the Evening Star, Joseph Noel Paton

8   Wild im Winterwald, Arthur Thiele, 1874

10 Lamia, John William Waterhouse

12 Spring, John Collier

14 Sir Galahad and the Angel, Joseph Noel Paton

16 Earrings, William-Adolphe Bouguereau, 1891

18 Cupid and Psyche, William-Adolphe Bouguereau

20 Joan of Arc, Paul de La Boulaye, 1909

22 Beach Study, Henry Scott Tuke

24 Sleeping Beauty, Gustaf Tengren

26 The Shadow, Edmund Blair Leighton

28 Perkūnas, Mikalojus Konstantinas Čiurlionis

30 Adieu, Alfred Guillou, 1892

32 A Valkyrie, Edward Robert Hughes

34 Accolade, Edmund Blair Leighton

36 Spring Scattering Stars, Edwin Howland Blashfield

38 Boreas, John William Waterhouse

40 Under Eketreet, Hans Gude

42 The Angel of the Birds, Franz Dvorak

44 Erwachende Germania, Christian Köhler, 1849

46 Cupid and Psyche, William-Adolphe Bouguereau

48 The Shepherd's Dream, Johann Heinrich Füssli

50 The Cemetery, Caspar David Friedrich

52 Illustration from Richard Wagner's Tristan and Isolde, 1909

54 Tristan and Isolde, August Spiess

Printed in Great Britain
by Amazon